MODERN LUXURY

MODERN LUXURY

RICHARD MISHAAN

WRITTEN WITH ELIZABETH GAYNOR
PRINCIPAL PHOTOGRAPHY BY GEORGE ROSS
THE MONACELLI PRESS

Published in the United States by The Monacelli Press,
a division of Random House, Inc., New York.

The Monacelli Press and colophon are trademarks
of Random House, Inc.

Library of Congress Cataloging-in-Publication Data

Mishaan, Richard.
Modern luxury/Richard Mishaan.—1st ed.
       p. cm.
ISBN 978-1-58093-228-8 (hardcover)
1. Interior decoration. I. Title.
NK2110.M572 2008
747—dc22

2008045888

Printed in China

10 9 8 7 6 5 4 3 2 1
First Edition

Design by Doug Turshen

www.monacellipress.com

All photography by George Ross except the following:

Fernando Bengoechea, pages: 22, 60, 62, 83, 130, 131, 173, 174, 175, 189
Philip Ennis, pages: 105, 116, 178, 179
Josh McHugh, pages: 13, 149, 183, 184, 185, 199
Peter Peirce, pages: 57, 58, 59
Eric Piasechi, pages: 73, 74, 76, 77, 132, 133, 159
Marco Ricca, pages: 64, 65, 160, 190

I dedicate this book to my wonderful and whimsical family, Marcia, Nicholas, and Alexandra. I thrive on your energy. I love you all.

FOREWORD

PAMELA FIORI
EDITOR-IN-CHIEF, TOWN & COUNTRY

I have been trying to pinpoint the exact moment I met Richard Mishaan, but the truth is I can't remember. It wasn't more than eight or so years ago, but I feel as if I've known him forever. He is one of those men whose charm and exuberance are immediately evident, and they are probably two of the many reasons he has been such a success as a designer. But they are not, by any means, the only ones. Richard is a man of myriad interests and abilities and someone with endless curiosity. He named his first retail store Homer, after the artist Winslow Homer, whose work was prominently displayed next door at the Whitney Museum of American Art. When I asked Richard about the name, he said, "Winslow Homer's paintings are meant to wander off the page. Homer did this to provoke the imagination so that the viewer wonders what is happening in the area just beyond what he or she can see. Also, Homer's impressionistic style was new as well as rather avant-garde for its time. All of these elements are modern American and classic. That is what I wanted the shop to be." And that is exactly what it was.

I had a different impression about the store's name. Whenever I thought of Homer, I envisioned the Greek poet who wrote the *Iliad* and the *Odyssey* and that, to me, seemed to fit perfectly with Richard's aesthetic. Perhaps it's because there is something epic about his design sensibility. Richard doesn't think small—he is not a minimalist—when he does something, he goes all out with his enthusiasm. It was not long before that first store, featuring accessories and home furnishings on Madison Avenue, expanded into a showroom serving design professionals. And like Homer the poet, Richard Mishaan the designer is an adventurer—literally, because his travels take him to the world's most exotic, far-flung places for inspiration, and creatively, because his imagination knows no bounds or borders. In the space of a single room, for instance, he might include objects and furnishings from several different periods— Italian neoclassic, seventeenth-century French, Art Deco, and Biedermeier. In the hands of someone else, such a gathering might end up looking like the contents of a small museum's storage area. In Mishaan's hands, it not only looks as if it all belongs together but, more important, it is a beckoning environment that brims with personality.

The youngest of four siblings, Richard Mishaan was born in Colombia and lived there, on and off, for thirteen formative years. His mother was the child of Russian parents who fled there to escape World War II. His father, who emigrated to Colombia from New York, was initially involved in textiles, later branching out into other areas. The Mishaans came to be regarded as one of the most prominent families in Colombia and an integral part of the artistic community. They became good friends with, among others, the artist Fernando Botero, and became avid collectors—an avocation passed on to their son.

Richard attended Columbia University's Graduate School of Architecture in New York, but upon completion in the early 1980s found that there were few job opportunities for him due to the recession. Through a friend, he turned to women's fashion and eventually developed his own label. After working in fashion for several years, he grew disenchanted and decided to try his hand at home design. (He also was recently married and about to become a father.) He returned to Columbia University to take a degree in real estate development, and began his new and present life as head of his own company. That was 1992, and he has been at it ever since.

The Mishaan touch, stylistically, is an expansive one, which is not surprising—he himself is an expansive person. His combined knowledge of fashion, architecture, and interior design, plus his cultural roots, give him a deep understanding of luxury and quality, which is immediately apparent upon entering an apartment or house that he has designed. While he uses serious pieces and has a disciplined eye, there is also a playfulness about his work, sometimes in his overall compositions and at other times in the particular placement of a Lalique vase or cluster of tribal masks. Richard knows how to lighten up the atmosphere, as well as the spirits of those who inhabit it. You get the feeling that this designer likes to have fun in his own life and wants to impart a similar sense of joy to his clients.

As an art lover himself, Richard takes great pleasure and pride in working with clients who are collectors. Deciding where a canvas or a drawing will be hung or figuring out the exact surface upon which a sculpture should be displayed is of the greatest importance to him—not only so it can be viewed properly but so that it can be appreciated within the context of the space as a whole.

Richard is also a music lover and cites Stephen Sondheim's *Sunday in the Park with George* as one of his favorite plays. At one point, the George of the play—the nineteenth-century French neo-impressionist Georges Seurat—speaks of his craft: "The challenge: bring order to the whole. Through design. Composition. Balance. Light. And harmony." That also sums up Richard Mishaan's approach to interior design. I would simply add one thing: Have a wonderful time in the process. And that he most assuredly does.

INTRODUCTION

MODERN LUXURY is a celebration of the fusion-style interior design for which I have become known. My look has evolved over many years, since the first room I decorated for the venerable Kips Bay Boys & Girls Club Decorator Show House gave me a platform to demonstrate to a knowledgeable audience my belief that all good things can live together and enrich each other, regardless of style or period or price.

I have had the pleasure of working with clients whose informed taste in art and fine objects has permitted me to ▶

integrate wonderfully diverse collections into their homes. I am constantly being educated about prized possessions by their owners. Often, my view of objects for which I originally felt no affinity changes through proximity and the influence of cultured clients. My mission has been to create environments that provide a proper context for treasures amassed over lifetimes rich in travel, museum-going, antiquing, and gallery-gazing.

My eye has been made keener by my clients' collections and by my own travels. I was born in Colombia and educated in the United States. My orientation is global. Wherever I go, I find joy in understanding cultural differences, unearthing their artistic expressions, and bringing examples home. I am a born collector, like those for whom I often design.

I love nothing more than creating a cross-cultural dance among beautiful objects in my rooms—I am the choreographer who wants every member of his ensemble to shine. Home

design is like a performance. Or, liken it to a work of art. The end result, however, need not feel like a museum, so there is no reason to follow conventional notions of display. One of the pleasures of owning art and fine objects is that one can do things that curators and dealers would not, such as hang an Old Master painting on a frosted, mirrored wall, or suspend modernist drawings from the edges of bookshelves.

In the pages of this book you will see that I have no signature style. I love mixing things in unexpected ways. When asked how I use color, when I know to drench a room in neutral tones, or why I think a quirky piece makes a room, I find myself describing my work in paradoxes, such as "brazenly gracious" or "powerfully Zen."

I bring my sense of travel into play, not as a guide, but as a gypsy who has been seduced by the enchantment of each continent. I myself am a mix of exotic breeds. I think it shows in how comfortably I place a work by Fernando Botero next to a tribal piece.

HELLO FROM MY FRONT HALL, above. My Orion series Macassar ebony table, at right, has a showy starburst top and inlaid edge.

Art is one of my great loves. From my parents, I learned the determination to set my sights on good art that speaks to me. They taught me to collect from instinct and with passion. Art adds immeasurably to every design project, offering color, dimension, and humanity.

I was schooled in architecture and that background stands as the solid footing of my work. Everything begins with the proportions of a space. If they're wrong, no amount of decorating will put things right. Good architecture supports the scale of what comes next, the splendid amalgam of textiles, furniture, and other objects within a space.

Sometimes I imagine myself an anthropologist. Over the years, I have made a study of how people live. While my calling is primarily aesthetics-based, an equally important dimension of my work is organizing the flow of people's lives so they click within their habitat. This may mean reconfiguring a layout to correspond to real-time needs, whether it's making a spare bedroom into a gentleman's study or a lady's dressing room, or converting a breakfast room into a family computer lab.

And what of luxury? Luxury implies the highest level of quality, and quality is tied to authenticity, not showmanship. Truth of purpose and excellent workmanship are the prime ingredients in a successful room installation. By this I mean the care with which walls have been painted, sewing has been executed, floors have been finished, and moldings have been applied. From these treatments, I build layers and nuances that become more apparent the longer one experiences the space. Luxury can be revealed subtly through beautiful detailing and fine materials.

I discovered early on that the type of well-proportioned, well-made furnishings I wanted were not always available, so I began to design them. Many who know my custom furniture, first sold through my shop Homer, think of me as a modernist. Yet "modern" can conjure a less-is-more image that's not a complete picture of what I'm about.

My interiors are precise but layered, clean yet eclectic, contemporary but based in history, and always very today. I hope you will find in this book the same delight I take in living with beautiful pieces and arranging them as a means of personal expression. The greatest luxury of all is to spend your days surrounded by the people and things you love.

IN MY SHOP, I delighted in staging arrangements that translated to interior design concepts ready for use. Here, a pair of pony skin and bronze Parsons tables are matched by goatskin and iron stools, all by Hervé van der Straeten. Bronze and aluminum horns are by Chuck Price.

A FIRST IMPRESSION

An entrance hall is a gateway into someone's life. As a first glimpse of how a person presents himself or herself, it must be arresting and beautiful. I like to establish a client's design message up front—with color, the placement of art, or perhaps the way a door beyond captures the light and frames an adjoining room.

A foyer is uniquely suited to a kind of formality. There should be a degree of emptiness about the space because it's a place that people flow through. Very few elements are extraneous, so things placed there and the ▶

surface finishes you choose will attract attention and ought to be eye-catching. A stairway banister and newel post can be crafted as artistically as sculpture. The floor, the walls, the furniture, the artwork—all are essential parts.

Graciousness requires that the space be hospitable, planned with the idea of welcoming guests. The room speaks to the owner's identity. But the self-contained quality of a foyer, as a place unto itself, is freeing in a design sense. Here, I am at liberty to introduce, to amuse, to surprise. It's the perfect staging ground for stunning art and for unexpected visual connections.

A front hall has a job to do, but not at the expense of aesthetics. The necessities are a table where the mail is left and a surface to put down keys. Briefcases and shopping bags want a place under a table or console. People need convenient areas to hang coats and stash umbrellas. I prefer to offload utilitarian tasks at a secondary entrance, if available, so I can focus the "wow factor" to make a great impression in the formal entry.

Our own country house has a very large foyer that incorporates three areas of equal visual importance: a weighty Tuscan console table with a playful sculpture on it by Niki de Saint Phalle, a sweeping staircase, and an ornamental, eighteenth-century Swedish ceramic stove that stands on the deep umber-stained wood floor. The stove was my grandmother's, and it is full of meaning for me. After World War II she began her life anew, in Denmark. As long as I can remember, I've been going to visit family in Denmark, so Scandinavian blue-and-white porcelain is a big through-line for me. My grandmother loved that stove dearly; it heated her bedroom and made an indelible decorative statement. When I inherited it and the movers brought it to my house, they happened to set it down in the front hall, and it was as if the stove had claimed its rightful place. I love the serendipity of how that came to be.

I like to receive people in a grand way, but it's not about being grand. When we give cocktail parties, people love to cluster in our foyer. When there's music, it becomes a dance floor. On cold winter days when the kids were little, they skateboarded in this hall. There's a certain luxury in just having that space to use.

None of the objects in our front hall are technically related, but everything relates. The ingredients may appear to be random, but they were chosen with care. We've assembled pieces with personality that hint at ours. They are strong pieces that reinforce or offset each other but can also stand alone decoratively.

If design is done right, the elements of a room work well together without it being obvious why. Meaningful objects inevitably come into your life, and it is for you to define the proper associations among them. In an entrance hall, you can strikingly establish those relationships. You can also set the rapport you want your guests to have with your home. It's not essential that the front hall deliberately send a message about what's coming next. But, frankly, it always does.

FAUX-PAINTED LIMESTONE WALLS stand solidly behind a modern Louise Nevelson sculpture that balances an important classical arrangement: a console made for Napoléon Bonaparte, a marble torso by Fernando Botero, and eighteenth-century Italian urns. *Overleaf:* A minimally appointed foyer in a house modeled on a Parisian mansard mansion gives breathing room to a compelling combination of a French Empire table, a 1940s Daum crystal chandelier, and David Hockney's painting *Celia*. The Art Nouveau–inspired staircase railing echoes their curves.

FORCEFUL ARCHITECTURE CREATES a strong first impression in my 5,000-square-foot design studio with 14-foot ceilings. The reception area and front hall convey my eclectic style. The ebonized oak and steel doorway of the adjacent seating area frames the hall like artwork, above. At right, a 1930s cabinet mixes with wall sconces from the original Eden Roc Hotel in Miami Beach, a Sol LeWitt drawing, Japanese lacquerware, and Masai warrior masks. *Previous pages:* Surprise and serendipity are at play in cross-pollinating an antique Swedish ceramic stove with a contemporary sculpture by Niki de Saint Phalle and a Tuscan console table in the spacious entry of my own country house. *Overleaf left:* A quiet alcove waiting area, with a painting by Gustavo Acosta and lacquered wood garden seats by Thomas Boog, counters strong colors found elsewhere in my studio. *Overleaf right:* A red lacquer wall with recessed stainless steel baseboards is a bold foil for a 1930s-style French console, a mirror by Hervé van der Straeten, a Royal Copenhagen porcelain bear, and contemporary French pottery. Clay busts atop steel I-beams are by Mexican artist Javier Marín.

I love an entrance that gives you a big hello every time you walk in. Hanging an important piece of art right up front is a great welcome, for both you and your guests.

A SMALL FOYER IN A MANHATTAN pied-à-terre is enhanced with faux-painted porphyry columns banded in stainless steel. An acrylic console and a mirror yield to the impact of Picasso's *Seated Blue Woman* and a Fernando Botero sculpture. *Overleaf left:* A Julio Larraz painting and Manolo Valdés bench sculpture command attention in a maple paneled second-floor hall where a nineteenth-century English lantern hovers over contemporary fittings. *Overleaf right:* In a collector's apartment, a cove ceiling crowns an energetic display of art and decorative elements. A Julio Larraz oil painting, Christo renderings, and a nineteenth-century Russian reception table are juxtaposed with faux marble woodwork and a marble checkerboard floor.

THE GRACIOUS ROOM

Bringing grace to life is the secret to living well. What exactly is being gracious? It is extending courtesies with charm, good taste, and a generosity of spirit. A living space that is perfectly in tune with how someone wishes to live reflects such grace. In grand gestures and small touches, a well-thought-out room extends a feeling of luxury to both you and your guests.

As the main entertaining areas in a home, living and dining rooms deserve pride of place. In the old-fashioned sense, these are areas where ▶

people are cued to be on their best behavior, setting the tone for visits. A gracious room should live up to these expectations and be decorated to share the owner's finest possessions with friends and family. But the finest can take many forms. An arrangement of miniature lighthouses collected on seaside vacations may be as seductive as an important painting on the wall, if it is handled imaginatively and is true to the spirit of those who live there.

Public rooms offer the most space for furniture and display. Mixing styles and scales generates interest. I believe that all good things can coexist and complement each other. There are design elements that link eighteenth-century antiques to Art Deco, modern, and so on, which can be analyzed and used to explain why pairings work. Yet cohesion is often something that's best felt and not intellectualized.

Regardless of style or cost, a piece's true value lies in its authenticity, in its flawlessness as an expression of its period, the material from which it's made, or the role it's meant to play. When objects are equally worthy in this sense, they create their own compatibility. Compatibility among disparate pieces of good value and design both stimulates and satisfies the eye.

Main living spaces can be very layered, very detailed, and as complex or simple as taste and space dictate. Quality materials convey luxury quietly. It is generous to incorporate some degree of *luxe*, whether in the wall coverings, textiles, or wood types selected. I gravitate toward exotic woods and like to allow their veining to create natural patterns for a flourish. For example, I may situate graining to travel up a credenza or to point in different directions, creating geometric patterns that bring excitement to a piece of cabinetry. I pay attention to these details and treat every feature of the room with the same importance.

Living rooms must be elegant but at the same time offer a level of comfort so people can gather with ease. Comfort makes us feel cared for and luxurious. A living room should welcome two guests or accommodate twenty-five equally well. Furniture arrangements that break seating into smaller groupings, so you can cozy up to intimate conversations, help achieve those ends. At the end of the day, when you are alone with a newspaper and a cocktail, you also want to feel drawn into your living room to relax.

In a dining room, it is acceptable to make the grand gesture. I like to appoint the table with great attention behind closed doors when I am setting up for a party, then open the doors only when it is time to dine. Guests should gasp at the beauty of the room and the tabletop. A table is a natural stage for amusing and engaging all five senses. A dining room presents an opportunity for a bit of theater.

Although my goal is elegance, I take care not to make a space so precious that people hesitate to use it. Why spend a fortune on a painting and then hang it in a living or dining room that is seldom entered? Always consider yourself as special as any guest. Rooms should be inviting enough that you want to use them on your own, with family, or with company. Life should be a celebration.

IN A LIGHT-FILLED DINING ROOM, warm tones promote compatibility among a grab bag of styles that include an Art Deco table and chairs, an intricate gilded wood Biedermeier chandelier, a cabinet with brilliant marquetry in the style of André-Charles Boulle, Daum and Lalique crystal vases, a contemporary painting by Rufino Tamayo, and a Fernando Botero sculpture—all grounded by a colorful marble floor.

PICKING UP A SAVONNERIE CARPET'S COLORS while blatantly contrasting with its delicacy, a pair of Botero paintings anchors neutral upholstery and contrasting table styles— a Napoléon III against the wall and an André Arbus in the middle. A Barry Flanagan horse sculpture and chinoiserie porcelains are among the room's other appointments.

AN ACANTHUS LEAF PATTERN damask bathes dark woods in golds and yellows in a rich-toned dining room setting. Above, a painting by Julio Larraz floats over a Russian Empire console table displaying accessories that mimic the canvas's shapes and colors. A Venetian candlestick by Archimede Seguso completes the arrangement. At right, a formal still life painting by Claudio Bravo inspires accoutrements including a 1930s Venetian glass chandelier that once hung in the Lido nightclub in Paris, Russian Empire chairs, and a Daum vase.

I think of a space with some drawbacks as a cue to let my imagination soar. For example, high ceilings in a small room offer a chance to draw the eye upward. Curtains that drape gracefully just below a ceiling line can change everything.

A NARROW ROOM WITH SOARING HEIGHT gets a lift from ceiling-high quilted drapes, turning a deficit into an asset. Chocolate curtains frame a pale blue sofa served by a bronze drum table and a pair of shagreen taborets to create an inviting window seat. *Overleaf left:* A shared simplicity unites objects from across the centuries. A large 1950s color-field painting by Jules Olitski, a torso from the first century, a quartz Art Deco–inspired bowl by Henry Dunay, and a Russian Empire console grace a living room. *Overleaf right:* It's all about shine. Walls covered in silver-thread grass cloth and seating in Bergamo silks lend soft sheen to a setting that glimmers with a 1930s antiqued Venetian mirror, mirrored two-tier coffee table, and crystal accessories.

Silhouettes pop when you inject dark woods into a pale neutral setting. It's a way of creating contrast quietly, establishing tranquility.

A TOWNHOUSE WITH LOFTY CEILINGS is treated to a creamy palette to highlight umber-toned Deco-style chairs, a French Art Deco Macassar ebony commode, and a parchment-covered drum table. The silk carpet's design recalls the patterning of beach sand as the ocean recedes.

POSITIONING A CONTEMPORARY SETTEE in the window and making use of clear occasional pieces—like a Venetian glass table lamp and an acrylic and chrome side table by Phyllis Rowen—expands space in a modestly sized living room. Strokes of dark brown in the coffee table, chair frames, and button tufting on one of my sofas punctuate the neutrals.

A PEDESTAL TABLE by Karl Springer and Russian Empire chairs graciously turn the entry of a living room into an area for games, light meals, or a cocktail buffet. Pieces of such stature are complemented by important art and accessories: an impressionist painting by Maurice Utrillo, a Botero painting, a gold leaf horse sculpture by Goudgi, and a gilt-lined repoussé bowl. Slate floors and faux-painted porphyry columns frame the arrangement.

A FINE ART COLLECTION GETS STAR BILLING in a modern living room wrapped in museum-gray walls and charcoal gray mohair seating. Paintings are hung on a frosted, mirrored wall over an L-shaped banquette accented with metallic silver pillows. When the sun sets, the west-facing space glows red, picking up shades in the paintings. In one corner, above left, the delicate lines of a table by Diego Giacometti contrast marvelously with a pair of Botero's hefty ladies, his marble sculpture, and an equally full bouquet of peonies.

IN A MEDIA ROOM, a straight-forward layout orients seating toward screens. Simple upholstery emphasizes the room's art and allows disparate objects to shine. Biedermeier chairs, a Karl Springer two-tiered coffee table, and a modular 1970s banquette stand on a crimson carpet. Art includes a bronze torso by Alexander Archipenko as well as a sculpted head and the painting *Mona Lisa* by Botero. A table is placed in the window to profit from natural light and the view.

PERCHED HIGH IN A NEW Manhattan tower, this living room's light-filled space is enhanced by a latte color scheme. Red is used judiciously to punctuate the calm. A two-tiered coffee table efficiently organizes books and showcases a sprocket sculpture. Paintings by Luis Chan and Zahara Schatz marry well with a bronze sand dollar sculpture and with the form and color of a traditional Japanese figurine.

Clean lines without fussy ornamentation invite the eye to explore details, and nuances surface.

IN A SPACE DECORATED for a Kips Bay Show House to do triple duty as a den, home office, and media room, maize fabric stretched on the walls reiterates the tone of the pale oak hearth. A floating glass shelf stands in for a mantel while an unframed mirror, glass accessories, and transparent table join to keep the space light in feeling.

FURNITURE OF VARYING HEIGHT and different shades of brown creates interest and warmth in this room broken into distinct areas for conversation, games, media viewing, reading, and work. Above, settees by Olivier Gagnère were inspired by eighteenth-century shapes. The pouf and side chairs are by Eric Schmidt, and a large painting from Donald Baechler's "Sundae" series adds an amusing touch. Dramatic bamboo cut-out lights at right are Balinese and the cachepot is by Hervé van der Straeten.

LAYERS OF PATTERN maintain the rich visual wrap on one side of my living room, from Nevelson's evocative construction, which fills the wall behind the sofa, to the Tibetan carpet and velvet faux tiger pillows. Solid shapes in ivory and dark brown seating float lightly about the room. Manolo Valdés's *Meninas* figurine stands on a side table; Chuck Price's bronze wishbone rests lightly on the coffee table.

MIXED MEDIA COHABIT comfortably. Contemporary upholstered shapes join a nineteenth-century farm table, a Gothic pedestal table, and Murano black glass lamp. The rug, designed by my wife, Marcia, is a modern take on a traditional Tibetan tiger print. *Overleaf:* A living room set up for a summer rental sports navy and white in a sea of neutrals. The scheme gains distinction as a trove of one-of-a-kind objects, like a nineteenth-century twig mirror and leather directors' chairs.

A CHOCOLATE VELVET sectional sofa teams with a barklike patterned silk carpet to ground a framed series of Marilyns from *The Last Sitting* by photographer Bert Stern. Distinctive tables display art and flowers: the Pace coffee table once belonged to Francesco Scavullo, the blond wood end table is by Jay Spectre, and the table at left holds a Chuck Price bronze wishbone sculpture.

GUTSY INDIGO-DYED BAMBOO GRASSCLOTH mutes the walls of a media room enough to enhance viewing. A pair of American Empire chairs get a contemporary facelift with a geometric woven fabric that repeats the blue, as does a large serigraph by Manolo Valdés. A Tommi Parzinger table lamp forms a strong vertical line near mirrored shelves that climb the walls. Crystal votives are by Tony Duquette.

BOLD STROKES

Step out of the realm of good breeding for a moment, where bold often means brazen, and consider it as a design concept. To be bold is to be fully committed. For me, it is about acknowledging the level of excitement I feel in a space and allowing my design to reflect that. When I sense a strong connection to something, I follow my heart. The integration of that passion into my interior design is not work. It is what feeds me.

Using lots of color or lots of pattern makes a room pop. If I love a color, I go with it for ▶

the vibrancy I am after. Not committing to a color, a location, or an object compromises its integrity in the work. To be tentative about any of these elements would be to fall short of my intention. Remarkably, when there is a lot of one color in a room, it can act as a neutral. It is the same with pattern—the more there is, the less distracting it becomes. The eye begins to read continuity and doesn't alight on any one patch. In a room that is saturated, more is less. When a scheme is not so busy, individual items can draw undue attention, throwing off the feel of the room as an overall tapestry. Context is everything.

A stunning object or piece of furniture can make a bold statement through its sheer presence. My aim is to place it near other elements or against a backdrop that transmits the same level of energy, to support it. It's like a theater production, a dance performance, or a good piece of music. Once you incorporate a star element, everything else needs to be brought up a notch.

Simultaneously, I try to instill the spirit of Zen in my work; it lends strength to a room. In a design context, Zen translates to the balanced energy I strive for. Where elements are in balance, nothing is jarring. The overall effect, in fact, is one of calm. It is entirely possible to use strong color and intricate patterning and achieve this harmony. Buddhist cultures make generous use of color. In India, people and their homes are dressed in oranges and curries. In China, reds and golds are everywhere. Westerners often dilute the palette and potential of Zen.

If one style predominates in a room, it just dulls down the entire design scheme. Contrast stirs things up. In my studio, there is a pedestal table of my design—one of the most precious pieces I own—that I use for presentations and meetings. The detailing is superb. It's made of Macassar ebony, with a high-gloss finish that gives it a very 1940s kind of glamour. The legs are fluted and sit on pedestals trimmed in bronze. Above it, I've hung a cluster of inexpensive Chinese metal lanterns with cutout motifs, which I found on one of my trips to the Far East. That's bold. Massing the lanterns increases their design impact and perceived worth, but the high contrast between table and light fixture, in style and provenance, creates tension. Tension breeds excitement.

I have made it a point to design my studio so that it conveys the same energy I bring to any residential project. It is a showcase for the scale, quality, excitement, and intention I bring to my interiors. When clients come there for a meeting, they experience the strength of my work. Bold design draws attention to the moment. Bold expressions can be both energizing and serious. My work is high frequency, yet it is always welcoming.

VIBRANT SEASIDE TONES energize the living room of a traditional Hamptons Shingle Style home. Khaki softens formerly stark white walls. Bamboo chairs, a charity auction find, pull up to modern chrome tables by a graphic fireplace arrangement. The hearth centers this secondary seating area, but refreshingly, does not dominate the room. Sculpture by Balthazar Lobo.

A COOL-AS-A-WAVE Dorothy Draper sectional sofa in swimming pool blue throws a curve in a traditional setting that includes Louis XV–style chairs recovered in a David Hicks geometric print, a Chinese-inspired table, and a suede-trimmed charcoal sisal rug. Varied window treatments—shades as well as curtains—relax the room.

MY CHAIN PRINT WALLPAPER DESIGN inspired by a Jackie O link bracelet, above, reiterates sea colors on a dark brown background. Lucite directors' chairs and a 1970s table, together with a pale grass rug, bounce beach light around a den. In a dining room, right, a farm table is painted black to give it the strong silhouette of a paper cutout. Other furnishings contribute to the room's theme of stark contrasts, and red lacquer pedestals topped with gourd-shaped vases add pop.

IN A DINING ROOM of a different stripe, right, wood is offset by the intense red of a lacquer table by François Champsaur that commands attention. Grass cloth fills wall space between applied wooden strips; a starburst mirror by Hervé van der Straeten breaks visual boundaries and focuses the eye. Crisp white leather slipcovers on dining chairs add an additional layer of *luxe*. *Previous pages:* An explosion of color at ankle level counters the mass of a wooden ceiling in a modern dining room with a Zen feel. Christian Liaigre's sleek plum and chili pepper table sits on a sumptuous Tibetan silk carpet. Ingo Maurer's lighting hovers delicately above.

I ACQUIRED A FEW FANTASTIC PIECES by the late Tony Duquette, set designer and master of faux, for my country house dining room. Striped curtains bookend his amazing shell-encrusted console and mirror, above. Painted resin pagodas, also by Duquette, and candlesticks by Tommi Parzinger enhance its theatricality. At right, Duquette's fanciful twig, crystal, and resin chandelier hangs above a white lacquer dining table of my own design in a mix-and-match setting that incorporates a pair of fifteenth-century Gothic windows—intended for William Randolph Hearst's San Simeon estate—and a limited edition 1950s Royal Copenhagen china set.

FAUX MALACHITE WALLS, A FAVORITE Duquette treatment, show off his marvelous wire
chair and oversized resin shell planters in my shop, above. At right, Duquette's
resin snail lamp and metal table embedded with shells keep company with a series
of original costume drawings for a 1940s production of *Camelot*.

I want paintings and artful objects to take center stage. I let other materials—wood, metal, glass—bask in their refracted glory.

YACHT STYLE DEFINES THE CRISP, colorful look of a 3000-square-foot living space were tables break up the use of the space for the occasional light meal or game. Honey-toned paneling enhances the vibrant colorplay among a David Hockney watercolor, a patterned Dhurrie rug, and Olivier Gagnère vase. The table and chairs are reproductions of 1930s designs by Jean-Michel Frank.

AN IMAGINATIVE MIX OF PRINTS on a set of Karl Springer chairs is set off against a striped rug, above. Pattern on pattern is quieted by the mysterious subject matter of a Julio Larraz painting. The eye reads layered patterns as well in a mix of Renzo Mongiardino–style marquetry, Karl Springer stools, Lalique crystal, colored glass, and mirrored reflections in a bar that presides over an entire wall, right.

ANIMAL PRINTS FEEL LIKE NATURAL NEUTRALS in a living room, left. Tiger stripes appear on Italian Empire chairs and pillows, and faux zebra skin becomes a carpet. Tapestry-like drapes and Donald Baechler's expansive work on paper maintain the wrap of pattern. In a library, above, a bold medley of color and print continues with a Hockney silkscreen, Julio Larraz oil painting, Pierre Chareau table, and spikes of hot color from the coral and calla lilies.

In a dark interior, there must be pale furnishings and reflective surfaces—glossy woods, metallics, mirrors—to bounce light around and create shine.

STRONG LINES ARE MUTED BUT LUSCIOUS in a chiaroscuro scheme of chocolate and silver in the seating area of my loft. My Spider Chair pulls up to a silk velvet sofa where pillows covered in metallic threads softly reflect the light.

THROUGHOUT MY STUDIO, STRONG CONTEMPORARY FORMS are joined by unexpected pieces such as a Biedermeier cabinet and reproduction neoclassical statuary, above. In my design room, right, a grouping of metal lanterns found in China repeat the circular form of a mirror I framed with an industrial gear. Reflections in the highly polished table magnify the effect. *Overleaf:* This table is a meticulously detailed composite of sleek 1940s Art Deco lines that I interpreted in Macassar ebony. Chairs in the style of André Arbus add a second layer of shine to the space.

AN ANTIQUE JAPANNED CHEST atop an intricately carved silver-leaf wooden base steals the show in an elegant gray dining room while an esoteric combination of furnishings affords balance: an Art Deco–style table by Raymond Subes, a Buccellati silver candelabrum, and an abstract painting by Milton Avery.

A ROOM THAT WORKS

Form does follow function. Taking it further, function can drive design toward originality and excellence. I find as much reason to create thoughtful, luxurious design in a "practical" space as anywhere else in the house. Yesterday's dens, for example, are today's libraries, media rooms, and home offices—or all three. The information tucked away there is now digital as well as printed, and ingenuity is called for to reconcile the two agreeably.

A library or study should be a room that feeds the soul. I want to envelop my clients—literally ▶

and figuratively—in the books and music and artwork that nurture them in quiet moments. I like to wrap these rooms in two or three walls of beautifully crafted cabinetry. I believe in installing as many bookshelves as a room can hold, right up to the full height of the ceiling, while leaving one wall free for seating.

Bookshelves become archives of our interests and life experiences. In addition to housing the volumes we love, they should display meaningful objects and mementos. Integrating sculptures or treasures from past travels among books allows spontaneous memories of small delights to resurface. Layering makes a library rich. I place objects or photographs between and in front of books. I hang paintings directly from shelf edges, over some of the volumes, to create a kind of mosaic. For me, art is everything and I encourage people to pile it on.

In the study at my loft in downtown Manhattan (my summit room), I've filled the bookshelves to brimming with design and art books, magazines, ceramic containers, *objets d'art*, and the occasional African mask. I interspersed burnished brass swirl sculptures to do the job of bookends. In front of all of it, I've hung an enormous mirror framed with a turn-of-the-century mechanical gear. It's a patinated industrial piece that brings texture, shine, and an unexpected scale to my library.

I gravitate toward dark woods for cabinetry in a library or media room. Shelves, tables, and desks have a very strong presence when crafted from a fine wood that has been given a glossy French polish. The material is luxurious, and when colorful objects and art are played off against it, the counterpoint adds great punch. I also like to integrate a flat screen television into shelving. The shelves frame the screen, and the digital imagery adds life to the woodwork and volumes.

As a designer, one of my tasks is to organize a client's possessions in a personally expressive way and another is to lay out a home to be in synch with how its owner actually lives, or wishes to. All of us now multitask our way through our days and our rooms, so even the most beautiful library—or kitchen, bedroom, or master bath for that matter—must be able to function in versatile ways, often incorporating electronics.

Desks have a place in all kinds of rooms because of the ubiquity of the computer. I design for their presence in libraries, kitchens, and kids' and adults' bedrooms. I like to install filing cabinets and drawers for the storage of documents elsewhere, in a dedicated office or study, in order to maintain clean, occasional work surfaces that will not invite clutter in these alternative workspaces.

I embrace technology and take the attitude that it deserves to stand proud in virtually any room. The idea of camouflaging electronics or hiding them away is outdated. I select the sleekest computers, televisions, sound systems, and speakers I can find so they may take their rightful place among other well-designed furnishings in a sophisticated environment, without apology.

IN A HOME LIBRARY, small framed pieces form an artful background for reading or study. A pedestal table and chairs by French designer Jules Leleu are situated near works by Jean Cocteau, Sol LeWitt, Alex Katz, and others. Major art is layered over full-to-brimming bookshelves and treated in a relaxed way.

AIRY SHELVES OF MY DESIGN in grainy zebrawood with bronze detailing stand up to other good cabinetry and Art Deco–inspired furniture. At left, they bookend a desk in the style of Jean-Michel Frank and a side chair by Ruhlmann that integrate a workspace into a living area. Butterscotch walls and large-scale art warm up the dark wood. Above, a collection of old and new Royal Copenhagen porcelain finds a place in the same shelf unit used elsewhere in the room as it awaits a growing library.

FREESTANDING TABLES CREATE UNCLUTTERED, good-looking workspace anywhere there's a free corner in a living room or bedroom. For a distinctive Parsons table, above, I topped Macassar ebony legs with a laminated white parchment surface. The desk is accompanied by a pair of Giacometti-inspired chairs—flea market finds—that add a touch of artistry. Patrick McMullan's framed photography anchors the arrangement. At right, white dashed with black defines an occasional desk set-up in a master bedroom with a skyline view.

A SERIES OF BOTANICAL PRINTS provide a graphic backdrop to a crisp desk design in a chocolate brown room, left. Tall accessories visually tie the art to the work surface. A beaded curtain injects movement and light into the dark setting. Above, vertical shelves inspired by the work of Gerrit Rietveld are balanced by artwork that fills wall space over a corner desk. *Overleaf left:* In my design studio, a parade of vintage French Army cabinets topped by stacked boxes stand in for a sample room. A vintage lantern reiterates the strict geometry. *Overleaf right.* A large-scale mirror throws a curve to my library's straight lines; it is suspended directly from the shelves.

I embrace technology and take the attitude that it deserves to stand proud in virtually any room. The idea of camouflaging electronics or hiding them away is outdated.

THIS FAMILY MEDIA ROOM is often an end-of-day gathering place. Light upholstery and a gold-leaf ceiling give life to a setting where dark walls are essential. A flat screen television is hung from a mahogany wall that also supports a system of wooden L-brackets and glass shelves mounted up to the moldings. *Right and overleaf:* A casual lineup of laminated fashion photos tops the media cabinet.

MY COUNTRY HOME'S LIBRARY is my favorite room in the house. It is equally welcoming for a sole reader or for a group of friends gathering for drinks before dinner. The room is cozy and graciously satisfies our appetites for books, artwork, comfortable seating near the fire, and a bar. A changing collection of framed photography leans against the base of the bookcase wall to bridge the transition from cabinet to carpet. The painting over the mantel is by Julio Larraz; the art just below the ceiling line is by Bryan Hunt.

TWENTY-FIRST CENTURY MEDIA ROOMS can be just as elegant as nineteenth-century libraries. The media unit in Macassar ebony, above, was designed to house the room's electronics, yet has the elegance of a fine credenza. Paneling the wall in the same wood visually ties in the flat screen television mounted there. At right, the dark surroundings required for optimal screen viewing are played off against glass and metal to add an element of sophistication. Shelves, a 1930s French radiator cover by Raymond Subes I used as a console in a shallow space, and a Tommi Parzinger lamp create points of light.

PRIVATE SCREENING ROOMS are no longer rare luxuries, but familiar gathering places for family and friends. Comfortable seating is crucial, as are small tables for light meals. Here, an assortment of unmatched tables and ottomans—in lieu of a single coffee table—can be pulled around to meet the needs of viewers. Sculpture and paintings balance the assemblage of furniture and electronics.

A STRIPED RUG AND COLORFUL UPHOLSTERED CUBES add a playful note to a young family's media room. The 14-foot sofa and roomy club chair by Patrick Naggar accommodate a full house. The sleek speakers are left in full view—their wood tones are right at home with the seating's cocoa and chocolate hues.

PRIVATE LIVES

Bedrooms are our most personal spaces. We retreat there for privacy, for intimacy, and to withdraw from the world and replenish ourselves. In the bedroom, personal comfort is everything. I design bedrooms that manage to indulge a bit of visual fantasy as well as accommodate a client's occasional need for a quiet space to work. Often, bedrooms must provide for a couple with different habits, so both sets of wishes must be blended harmoniously.

I address the comfort factor first by selecting as large a bed ▶

as the room can hold. I prefer upholstered beds with the hand of an interesting textile and the cushioning of a fine piece of overstuffed furniture. The prominent placement of an upholstered headboard in an alluring fabric immediately glamorizes the space.

I like to have at least six pillows on a bed, for the fullness of the look and to facilitate every kind of relaxation. At various times, you want to be able to sit up and read, to fall back and recline, or to lie down and sleep. An ample supply of pillows fulfills all those needs. Plenty of pillows also come in handy for a couple whose children pop into bed with them on Sunday mornings or late at night when they're not feeling well—like mine.

The core of the room is the primary element: the well-dressed bed. Yet contemporary reality dictates that most bedrooms incorporate a television and a small desk or table as a place to organize and do paperwork. A bench is indispensable, at the foot of the bed or wherever it will fit, for putting on shoes or packing for a trip. For a woman, a dressing table is a welcome indulgence, perhaps tucked away in a setback or along a passage to the master bathroom. If space is tight, a makeup table can be designed to double as a spot for correspondence.

There is no greater opportunity for decorating to cater to well-being than in private quarters. I like to imbue a master bath with a spa quality where "clean" is the message, echoed by spare elegance. I love to incorporate a full sitting room, with a love seat and a small table for light meals, into a bedroom that's large enough. Couples crave a place to steal away from family demands now and then. These areas also allow one person to sit and chat while the other dresses before going out—a capsule of time together behind closed doors.

A bedroom should have the potential to morph into a cool retreat. There ought to be shades to draw that will dim daylight for a siesta on a summer afternoon. Quiet color also helps achieve a feeling of escape. I sometimes leave the floor bare around the bed or take up rugs seasonally just to create that wonderful quality of cool floorboards against bare feet.

The master bedroom in my country house is perfect for siestas. It was inspired by one of my favorite destinations, the Hotel Excelsior on the Lido in Venice. I covered my bedroom walls with Fortuny fabric in a shade of goldenrod, emulating the hotel's grandeur, which can feel sunny in daylight but amazingly shady and conducive to rest when the blinds are closed. In the center, I've hung a marvelous Venetian glass chandelier, an elaborate piece usually associated with a dining room. Opening my eyes to it in my bedroom is like waking to a dream.

LOTS OF PILLOWS AND UNDRESSED WHITE LINENS create a cocoon of this bedroom, where a roomy two-tiered night table and lap desk make the bed a place for easy reading or writing. A large framed mirror extends the motif of fresh whites and dark wood accents.

LARGE EXPANSES OF PALEST CELADON GREEN sumptuously accented with a chocolate seal throw, left, make for a comforting and glamorous retreat. Antique velvet glides over the headboard, coverlet, and a tufted bench with acrylic legs. A silk carpet continues the theme of plush fabrics. Above, a seating area includes a fanciful 1930s chrome table and a chair I designed after those on the *Normandie*. Mixed materials create subtle texture in this room of solid shades.

OUR MASTER BEDROOM SUITE IN THE COUNTRY conjures a stay in Venice. Using related fabrics on the walls, tray ceiling, and for the shades and drapes creates a luxurious feel and makes this room a haven for us. The sun-colored woven textiles set the room aglow. The damask is Fortuny, the Murano glass chandelier is by Archimede Seguso, and the paisley upholstered bed is by Angelo Donghia.

POLKA DOTS AND SCROLL PRINT UPHOLSTERY give a jaunty spin to an all-white bedroom where inherited furniture wanted reviving. Simple red accessories plus a little detailing go a long way. Above, red and black ribbon borders accentuate the lines of linens and curtains. At right, red paint enlivens a bamboo chair and a trunk in a niche outfitted with a desk.

I like using things in large numbers and I love repetition—as in poetry when a word is used over and over again to bring a point home.

IN AN OTHERWISE BLACK AND WHITE SCHEME, dolphin blue lacquer walls add punch. Here, the sitting area of a large bedroom is made orderly with the squared-off lines of the furniture and the photograph frames, which show to advantage against the walls. Zebra stripes and chinchilla pillows offer graphic exotica.

WHITE BECOMES POWERFUL in contrast to this strong blue. A bedside still life of a Murakami toy, earthy-but-elegant crystal table lamp, and a bouquet of peonies create an amusing focal point. I designed the bed and table; the lightning bolt prints are by Chuck Price.

A BOY'S ROOM IS minimally appointed to leave ample floor space for play. Simple furnishings will allow the room to mature with him. Real art, crafts, and meaningful mementos—rather than juvenile decorations—find a place on the walls.

A SAUCY SHAG RUG anchors fun furnishings for a teenage girl, including Emilio Pucci print pillows, a B&B Italia swivel chair, and an iron four-poster bed. Behind the bed's pillows, a long turquoise bolster softens the metal headboard.

SIMPLICITY REIGNS IN TWO BATHROOMS composed of straight lines and unadorned primary materials—concrete, stone, glass, and mosaic tiles. The message is "clean." At right, a freestanding, glass-walled shower in an airy master bath has a bench that traverses the shower's boundaries and can be used wet or dry.

THE COLLECTED ENVIRONMENT

Rooms need relationships. Otherwise, they appear to be merely accidental assemblages or simplistic exercises in matching. It is fundamental to establish associations among the furnishings, art, and objects accumulated over time. All good pieces can work together regardless of their period or provenance. I derive a deep satisfaction in helping others discover the freedom to meaningfully—and playfully—exhibit their possessions.

I play the role of curator. I sift through collections that clients have assembled during their ▶

travels through the world and through life, and organize pieces into dynamic relationships with each other. At the same time, analysis of a client's current lifestyle helps define a workable plan to ensure that a room will be grounded and comfortable as well as good-looking.

The best interiors are layered and rich; a room's intricacy and sophistication spring from this. Good architecture is the ideal base layer. Wall treatments and decorative surfaces form the next tier, followed by furniture. Art and accessories are the final touch, infusing the environment with a jolt of energy. I adore creating synergy between collected pieces whose common thread is a tonality, a texture, or simply the excitement they evoke in the client who chose them.

In a collector's life, possessions are always vying for space. It's the most precious commodity, so achieving engaged coexistence is a challenge. My mission is to find the right context—a wall of color, gently filtered light, or a complementary medley of pattern—to create an atmosphere where every object or piece of art can be appreciated on its own and also draw life from those around it.

Personal collections require time to build, and they thrive in room to grow. They have the potential to impart a sense of motion to a room, like gallery exhibitions that continue to change. A collection must be arranged to be pleasing at any moment in time, even if it is not "complete" or expansive. In fact, a measure of emptiness in a space is a virtue in more than one way. It welcomes new additions, provides necessary voids where the eye can rest, and can draw more attention to an individual piece than it might receive if it were surrounded by multiple objects.

True collectors can't stop. They feel an emotional pull toward art and objects when they sense a strong connection. Seldom is an acquisition related to filling a physical need. It is passion-driven. An interior must remain fluid to absorb new treasures. I bought a Louise Nevelson sculpture, homage to Matisse's *Jazz*, on impulse at auction. It caught my eye in a gallery as I was running up the stairs to another meeting in the same building. I found the massive white piece at once soothing and electric. Astonishingly, I got it for less than the hammer price. Although I had bought it without a thought to where it would go and without measuring for space, it filled one whole wall of my living room almost exactly, and adds a great presence to the room.

Presence is key. My aim is to form relationships among equally present objects, to balance them with others of like energy. Patterns emerge as furnishings are assembled, and I use them as cues about which items to bring together. Repetition of a single characteristic—color, scale, finish, or texture—is often the glue that makes independent articles cohere.

Objects reinforce each other through their similarities, but their differences also stimulate the eye. One quirky item paired with others creates buzz. Overall harmony must not be sacrificed for effects, however. A room is like a musical piece: it's essential to orchestrate a satisfying melody, then integrate the peaks and valleys. One doesn't want to be always in the crescendo. There should be just enough tension in the music so that everything resonates.

VASES OF DIFFERENT HEIGHTS on a table in front of a color field painting create a three-dimensional composition that enhances each contributor. *Overleaf left:* Glass objects of like coloration but different scale form an unexpected still life on and under a table. *Overleaf right:* A wall painted citron with a turquoise border reads as art behind a charcoal drawing by Chuck Price and my monochromatic furniture, building up layers that enrich the clean space.

IN A COLLECTOR'S DINING ROOM, an ad hoc assemblage of art, accessories, and furniture creates a contemporary, salon feel that can change easily with new acquisitions. *Overleaf left:* A silkscreen by Donald Baechler dominates a small foyer where round forms link art, resin stools, and glass accessories. *Overleaf right:* A large painting by Richard Winters commands attention in a corner seating area. Intentionally mismatched furniture is eye-catching and relaxed.

A SERIES OF FRAMED PHOTOGRAPHS
by Massimo Vitali becomes a wall
covering, imparting character and
graphic order to a dining room
setting. A bright lacquer table and
Murano glass chandelier add a
whimsical touch. *Overleaf:*
Metallics rule a living room corner.
A Paco Rabanne screen hung as a
serpentine room divider and a
Julian Schnabel painting define the
space. Hard metal chairs by Billy
Haines are given soft chinchilla
seats, an unexpected contrast.

I am both a modernist and a classicist—I believe we can honor traditional style without living in the dusty past.

WHITE CABINETRY AND WOODWORK contrast sharply with paper-bag-brown walls, enhancing the impact of white accessories with strong shapes. The patterning of an African drum table complements the upholstery of a Donghia side chair. A Christopher Makos print with an emphatic message gives a graphic twist to the convention of hanging a family portrait above the fireplace.

SIMPLE FURNITURE DESIGNS AND MINIMAL ART reach across time to sit well together in a living room, above. At right, a limestone mantel acts as a traditional foil for a modern leather director's chair and garden ornaments are used as stand-ins—outside the fireplace—for andirons. A graphic painting that echoes the scale of the firebox and texture of the chair casually leans on the mantel.

A ROOM DESIGNED FOR a Kips Bay Show House contains appointments from every decade of the twentieth century. A Mondrian-like wall treatment, conceived as a paste-up composition in blocks of ultrasuede, enlivens the various shapes. Ink drawings, opposite, are by Al Held; the metal side table is by Eric Schmidt. Above, a beautiful console and silver tray with a few handsome pieces of glassware create an instant bar.

PROMINENT OUTLINES OF ORGANIC LAMP SHAPES and dark-stained furniture create a linear composition within an airy dining room, above. At right, ceramics that relate to each other through coloration and Art Deco inspiration are grouped to make a statement. A trio of vases top off the bookcase, breaking its straight lines, and a solitary piece is given pride of place on a 1930s pedestal.

A SET OF DOLLS that represent top fashion designers as seen through their own eyes form a collection that infuses a library shelf with humor. *Overleaf left:* A lightning bolt painting by Chuck Price, a pair of crystal votive candle-holders, and a chinchilla pillow are unlikely allies in creating graphic tension around a violet high back chair. *Overleaf right:* A beveled mirror and Lucite console playfully throw light into an apartment entryway. A pair of modern high back chairs found a permanent home in the hall after the family's Labradors claimed them for naps when they were temporarily set down there on delivery.

ART CAN SET THE TONE FOR A ROOM. *Las Meninas,* a seventeenth-century portrait of a Spanish princess and her maids of honor by Diego Velázquez, is used as a repeated theme in Manolo Valdés's work. His novel renditions of a historical subject parallel my sampling of classics in designing contemporary furniture. We both strip away ornamentation to reveal essential shapes, then rework subjects in new materials. Valdés's *Meninas* feel at home in my interiors. Above, his serigraphs grace a modern seating area with a sheepskin stool by Hervé van der Straeten. At right, his alabaster sculpture and more abstract painting blend seamlessly with a spirited traditional mix.

I find satisfaction in helping others discover the freedom to playfully exhibit whatever they own.

IN THE COUNTRY, I see my backyard as an outdoor room and allow my art collection to spill onto the lawn. Here, a cast concrete and bronze sheep by François-Xavier Lalanne looks right at home near the weathered loggia.

PIECES OF EQUAL ENERGY team up to create amusing still lifes in my country home: a Niki de Saint Phalle ceramic dog vase, Alexander Calder silkscreen and Alexander III–style French bureau, above; and Ilario Palacio's engaging horse painting, a 1950s lamp, and a Biedermeier table, right.

CLASSIC DECORATIVE DETAILS
THE HAMPTONS   KEN MILLER

WATERCOLOR TONES WARM an imaginary artist's atelier in a show house. Walls are covered in blue felt and "framed" with black moldings to give them definition. Art ledges, also called out in black, support a changing array of paintings in a relaxed way. Furnishings appear as volumes of varying texture and height against the comparatively flat display of artwork in this studio setting. *Previous page left:* Set designer and artist Tony Duquette's elaborate fool-the-eye creations transmute plastic into coral and resin into ivory pagodas. The fantastical mother-of-pearl mosaic console, mirror, and chandelier are all his creations. *Previous page right:* Duquette's carved and gilded rose cupboards stand in front of a basket weave indigo wood wall in my shop, Homer. The height of the sconces and accessories counterbalance the remarkable chests.

CONTEMPORARY FORM

Contemporary is a way of thinking, not a time period. I feel like a classicist in twenty-first century clothing, and that clothing is couture. As in couture, good lines and fine materials are the essence of a first-rate design. Pleasing proportion and careful detailing are nonnegotiable. My custom furniture incorporates historical references, but it is forward-looking.

Every designer is fascinated by favorite period styles—older expressions of design and architecture that inform current work. I am drawn to ▶

eighteenth-century court styles, Biedermeier, and French furniture of the 1930s and 1940s, to name a few. These are take-off points for me, fine silhouettes that have been time-tested and that call to me to refine and rework them. Artists also operate this way: they become attracted to particular forms, which they explore again and again in their work with the idea of creating something completely new.

My desire is to strip away the characteristics of a period look that appear heavy to a modern eye, to peel back the layers of detail and reveal inherently good lines in their purest form. What emerge are clean volumes and an emphatic expression of certain stylistic elements. I go to the heart of a piece and reinterpret it in exotic materials, unexpected finishes, or of-the-moment textiles. It is a way of reinventing something from the past and making it suitable for contemporary use.

For example, I was inspired by a Jean-Michel Frank stool that was the twentieth-century French designer's take on a Louis XIV bench. Frank reinterpreted the classic piece in sharkskin and added loose velvet pillows. In turn, I was prompted to create my own version of this same stool, one that would feel right for today. I used tight, tailored upholstery for a sleek look that is all-of-a-piece and can be moved about easily without losing any cushions, a modern convenience.

In another instance, I wanted to reference the starburst motif popularized in the 1930s in the design of a table. I was able to merge a fine polished wood—Macassar ebony, a type

often used in the period—with a form that is almost tribal. I manipulated the shapes of spheres and arches to develop an accompanying chair. The result is a mannered and original series I call Orion.

A love of materials and experimentation with new combinations led me to begin designing furniture nearly as soon as I opened my interior design office. My training in architecture and background in fashion gave me the assurance I needed. As my interior design projects became more serious and larger in scope, I repeatedly found that available furnishings were lacking the properties I wanted, such as larger scale and special finishes. So began my custom furniture work, and I soon found that there was a demand for it. My retail shop Homer—which I treated as a gallery or salon with installations of furniture, *objets*, and art—was born. Not only were the contents contemporary in nature but so was my attitude about selection and presentation.

Having a contemporary point of view can also mean intentionally juxtaposing elements. In my interiors, I enjoy mixing my own furniture designs with others, just as I have always done at Homer. My look is grounded in a lack of conventional ornamentation, and in opposition. Turning an African drum into an occasional table and pairing it with a modern chair is a contemporary approach to design. Unexpected combinations work when they have shapes in common and are balanced in scale. The success of a contemporary form or a contemporary interior is both about choosing what to include and what to leave out.

AN ARTISAN'S MIRROR IS A TWO-TONE TAKE on a classic starburst. It marries appealingly with a pair of 1950s side chairs upholstered in yellow ultrasuede; their striking, lean silhouettes balance each other. *Overleaf:* My Orion collection is at once classic, modern, and organic—an exploration of arcs and spheres. A starburst is interpreted in Macassar ebony on the top surface of the table while stainless steel shadows the base.

All designers are inspired by the past. My own vision is sometimes quite minimalist, a bit tribal, a bit Zen.

IN THE FOYER OF A NEW YORK TOWNHOUSE, I commingle updates of classic shapes. A demi-lune sofa is designer Andrée Putman's contemporary interpretation of an eighteenth-century settee. The piece is pared down but luxurious in its simplicity. A black pedestal table by Christian Liaigre has classic roots as well. Its lines are reiterated in an ultra-diminutive table by François Champsaur and a resin vase by Christian Tortu. The rug, by Emma Gardner, suggests the modernization of a striped folk runner.

I don't know if opposites attract, but I do know that there is nothing more thrilling than putting unlikely objects together in a way that enhances their unique qualities, allowing you to see them anew.

A CONTEMPORARY POINT OF VIEW invites a Murano glass lamp to accompany an Assam Buddha hand and modern glass vase atop a Gothic pedestal table.

DISPARATE ELEMENTS INCLUDE items from the nineteenth through twenty-first centuries, above. An unusual twig-framed mirror, a stunning lamp by Gio Ponti, and a stainless steel radio play on scale and rough-versus-smooth to make the combination work. An Art Deco cabinet, opposite, with Murano glass jars creates a compelling entryway arrangement. A panther in bronze, signed Cartier, picks up on the glint of a metal sunburst.

The look I want to create
is clean, simple, not obvious.
My hope is that interesting
details and luxurious finishes
reveal themselves slowly,
rather than overwhelming
you on the first take.

IN A CORNER OF MY COUNTRY HOME'S LIVING ROOM, shades of white unite simplified forms
that all borrow from classic styles: the love seat takes its lines from eighteenth-century
seating, the sofa has a contemporary roll-arm shape, the table is a Ruhlmann-like design,
the figurine an unadorned *Menina* by Manolo Valdés. The curves of Louise Nevelson's
marvelous carved sculpture provide a backdrop that ties these shapes together.

A PAIR OF 1920S-STYLE CHAIRS I reinterpreted in white leather to accentuate their lines stand near steel "X" tables in two heights by Ludwig Mies van der Rohe in my living room. I found the unmatched tables in a thrift shop and liked the sly contrast of using them side by side. An end table, opposite, with eighteenth-century lines is covered in ivory parchment, its skirt and legs molded in one piece, after a design by Jean-Michel Frank for Nelson Rockefeller's apartment.

STRAIGHT EDGES AND CLEAN LINES are the essence of modern in crisp black and white. Inspired by Jean-Michel Frank's shagreen redo of a Louis XIV bench, I updated the design again, for the twenty-first century, above, with ebony frame, leather upholstery, and a stainless steel base. At right, traditional nesting tables are refreshed with an ivory parchment surface. I love to use animal prints as a graphic, yet natural, accent.

THE GEOMETRIC PATTERN of a 1950s resin room divider is echoed in the shape of black and white furniture—all updates of 1930s pieces. Above, I've deconstructed a contemporary high-back chair, giving it two-tone upholstery in tweed with a white leather seat and an exposed wood frame that outlines its form. Multiple tables of different heights can slide under each other when not in use, creating a living tableau, opposite. The "X" lamp by Vincent Collin was found at Editions Limités in Paris.

Whether a piece was made in the seventeenth or the twentieth century, whether it comes from Paris or Peru, isn't as important as its integrity.

A SOFA WITH LINEN UPHOLSTERY and claret chenille seats is long and linear, answering the strong lines of the wood window frame in this seating area. Black lamp shades and picture frames punctuate the neutrals and serve as a link to the iconic leather Eames chair in the foreground.

A BOOKSHELF I DESIGNED in ebonized wood is at home either in a contemporary workspace or in a more conventional seating area, adding an airy vertical element to each. The mix of metal and wood modernizes the shelves' classic Greek key motif. Above, a glass stool from Henry Dean in Belgium and a rectangular floor lamp in wood and acrylic take their place in an amalgam of strong, independent shapes. At right, Eric Schmidt's fine-lined ironwork chairs sit atop a zigzag rug by Denis Colomb. Framed oversized playing cards visually balance the graphic floor covering.

MONOTONE SCHEMES HIGHLIGHT FORM. Above, an African drum table topped with glass reads as a textured cylinder next to a boxy chair by François Champsaur. An antique African measuring stick laid along the baseboard feels modern in their company. At left, a mahogany table of my design has a textured top, beveled edges, and squared-off, tapering legs—details that confer it a measure of quiet luxury. Leather side chairs join in the marriage of simple geometrics.

REPETITION ENHANCES THE STATURE OF BASIC SHAPES and is satisfying to the eye. Here, leather cocktail tables and milk glass stools are used in pairs while a parade of raspberry glass cachepots containing topiaries show well against the chocolate suede sofa. A striped rug gives direction and perspective to the whole.

SHOPPING SLEUTH

Since the beginning of human history, collecting has been the obsession of tribal kings, warring invaders, and conquering monarchs. Centuries later, as some of the treasures that had been amassed found their way into museums and galleries they gained exposure to the interested public. Today, we can expand our historical knowledge and train our eyes by visiting the institutions that are the repositories of this cultural richness. The ease of travel facilitates our access to ancient artifacts and exotic ▶

collections, and I expand my vision by exploring every chance I get.

The cross-cultural pollination evident in the display of such bounty serves as a model for my (albeit more modest) interior design aspirations. I have always been taken with the splendor of the mix. A public space like the Place de la Concorde in Paris, where the centerpiece of the graceful eighteenth-century square is an obelisk that once stood at the temple of Luxor, is a grand representation of the kind of counterpoint I love.

On a smaller scale, another iconic location for me is the jewel box of an apartment kept by Coco Chanel on the rue Cambon, also in Paris. Here, the renowned couturier intermingled seventeenth-century Chinese coromandel screens, Art Deco furniture, and French rococo mirrors with artful twentieth-century gem-encrusted birdcages and whimsical chandeliers to sumptuous, layered effect.

It has been my great fortune to have had many individual collectors as clients, challenging me to work skillfully with diverse treasures. Their collections—from Persian miniatures to contemporary photography—have amplified my awareness and fostered the pleasure I now feel when integrating pieces of cultural weight into elegant everyday interiors.

In the spirit of incorporating textured assemblages into all my work, I have honed my shopping skills to be on the lookout for both the historically significant and the unusual. There are many sources for such finds, such as the Gothic windows once used in William Randolph Hearst's home in San Simeon that I landed at auction, or a 1950s limited-edition Royal Copenhagen porcelain dinner service I ferreted out in a specialty antique shop, which seemed as if it were custom-colored for my own dining room.

My aim is to help clients get a knowing look at the assortment of things that are available to them and to help them develop a sense of how they wish to live in their homes. I urge people to challenge their imaginations by visiting museums, important antique shows, and auction houses to familiarize themselves with examples of fine craftsmanship so they can make informed purchases.

Once you've done your homework and have a feeling for the esthetics of what you're looking at, my advice is—unless you are shopping for investment purposes—if you love a piece, just buy it. In my early years of collecting, I found a colonnade sculpture in an out-of-the-way shop, a replica of a Greek ruin that gave my living room a dash of antiquity. One "expert" I met attributed it to an eighteenth-century studio. Later investigation proved it to be a production piece, a 1930s grand tour memento, one of about twenty made for first-class passengers on an ocean liner. Having it identified was informative and fun, and learning that the piece was of lesser value than I originally imagined did nothing to diminish my fondness for it and for what it did for my décor.

In this chapter, I make note of some favorite global haunts—venues grand and simple—that have helped me understand the amazing array of objects that have come down to us through history. Here is an informal list of places you can count on to educate your eye and refine your taste, as well as sources where you can discover and acquire treasures. No matter what their monetary value, personal finds will add the layering to your home that makes living there a luxury.

MUSEUMS

Museums can help improve your recognition of, and appreciation for, objects and art across a wide spectrum of historical periods. You get a comparison of the contributions of various cultures as well as a timeline, helping you to understand geographical and chronological origins. If you decide to collect more seriously, you can make valuable dealer contacts through curators and acquisitions committees.

IN AMERICA—New York: I never tire of the American wing or French galleries at the **METROPOLITAN MUSEUM OF ART** to refresh my view of period styles and see the best examples in context. At the **MUSEUM OF MODERN ART** design galleries, I love the industrial design from the twentieth and twenty-first centuries—from salad bowls to iPods—that boasts excellence in mass production and ergonomics. At the **NEW MUSEUM OF CONTEMPORARY ART** relocated on the Bowery, both the building's architecture and the international works by emerging artists push the envelope.

Los Angeles: The **ARMAND HAMMER MUSEUM OF ART AND CULTURE CENTER** presents key single artist, architect, and thematic exhibitions, which fill out my knowledge. The **GETTY CENTER** is as alluring for its stunning architecture and view over the city as it is for its international collection of decorative arts.

Washington D.C.: I am mad for the **PEACOCK ROOM**, once the sumptuous dining room in the London home of a wealthy shipowner from Liverpool, England, who commissioned James McNeill Whistler to adorn every surface. It's been recreated at the **FREER GALLERY OF ART** at the Smithsonian.

IN EUROPE—Paris: The **MUSÉE DES ARTS DÉCORATIFS**, housed in a wing of the Louvre, has the best survey of French furniture, porcelain, carpets, and displays of luxurious materials and their uses in the decorative arts. Special attention is paid to Art Deco, one of my favorite periods. Other sections of the **LOUVRE** are always worth a visit for both iconic and lesser-known European pieces. The **CENTRE GEORGES POMPIDOU**, or Beaubourg, holds great comprehensive shows on individual artists.

Copenhagen: The **DANSK DESIGN CENTER** gives a great overview of one hundred years of Danish design and the contributions of other heavyweight Scandinavian design stars.

Florence: The **PALAZZO PITTI** is a vast Renaissance palace near the Arno River that dates from the fifteenth century. It was eventually purchased by the Medici family, who used it as their chief residence. The structure showcases the architecture, landscape design, and fine art created courtesy of the patronage of this powerful family.

London: The **VICTORIA AND ALBERT MUSEUM'S** period rooms are outstanding, as are its enormous collections of furniture, glass, ceramics, and textiles, dating from the Middle Ages to today. The **TATE MODERN**, in a renovated power station in the heart of the city, is one of my favorites for British and international modern art from 1900 to the present.

Rome: The **BORGHESE GALLERY**, in an exquisite villa, houses a collection started in the seventeenth century by Cardinal Scipione Borghese, an early patron of Bernini and collector of Caravaggio.

IN RUSSIA—St. Petersburg: Two marvelous palaces outside the city are always worth a visit. The **CATHERINE PALACE** at Tsarskoe Selo, especially for its Chinese Hall, a treasure trove of Chinese ornamentation in enamel, porcelain, and safflower within walls covered with early eighteenth-century painted panels in ebony frames, and ceiling lusters made out of vases—all executed by Chinese workmen. **PAVLOVSK**, the palace built by Catherine the Great for her son Paul I, the ne plus ultra example of Russian neoclassical style, for both its elegant architecture and interiors. I would be thrilled to move right in and not change a thing!

ELSEWHERE—**BANGKOK, THAILAND: JIM THOMPSON** was an American entrepreneur who founded the Thai Silk Company. His compound of six traditional peaked teak houses is now a museum filled with a personal collection of antiquities from Southeast Asia and beautiful textiles to purchase. **BOGOTÁ, COLOMBIA: THE GOLD MUSEUM** has spectacular pre-Columbian art and tribal jewelry as well as ancient objects in ceramic, stone, and metal. **MARRAKECH, MOROCCO: THE MAJORELLE GARDEN**, an exquisite botanical garden designed by a French expatriate artist, and later acquired by Yves St. Laurent and Pierre Bergé. Villa rooms that Jacques Majorelle decorated in shades borrowed from his watercolors have been preserved. **XIAN, CHINA: MUSEUM OF THE QIN TERRA COTTA WARRIORS AND HORSES** is a structure built over an archeological dig that unearthed thousands of amazing life-size soldier, horse, chariot and other funerary statues dating from 210 B.C., which were buried with the first Chinese emperor.

AUCTION HOUSES

Auctions provide access to select personal collections of furnishings, and are often grouped into periods and styles. Catalogs are useful in giving you a feel for the relative values of objects in the current market. Generally, sales lots are on view for several days before an auction. Visiting these previews is a great way to learn about a style or a particular craftsman, or to evaluate prospective purchases.

If you are unable to attend an auction, many houses will accept bids by phone, absentee arrangement, or online. It may be worth inquiring the day after a sale to see whether the piece you had your eye on sold. If not, sometimes the owner will entertain a private bid below the stated minimum.

The list here purposely excludes the biggest houses, Sotheby's and Christie's, which are well known. In addition to my suggestions below, keep an eye open for regional auction houses. Especially in pockets of affluence and taste outside metropolitan areas, they can be great places to pick up well-priced quality pieces.

BONHAMS & BUTTERFIELDS AUCTIONEERS is the premier West Coast house, headquartered in San Francisco. Founded in the mid-nineteenth century, Butterfields originally targeted people moving to the area during the California Gold Rush, and now auctions fine art, antiques, and decorative objects. They were acquired by the British house Bonhams in 2002. I became acquainted with them when they handled the Halston estate.

GROGAN & COMPANY is a regional house located in Dedham, Massachusetts, outside Boston. They hold four large estate auctions each year with smaller specialty sales interspersed. I have found exceptional items from old line Boston families and posh Newport vacationers here.

RAGO ARTS AND AUCTION CENTER in Lambertville, New Jersey boasts excellence without attitude in its sales of twentieth-century decorative arts. This regional house draws antique dealers, designers, and collectors from New York and Philadelphia to its sales.

TAJAN, in Paris (with branches in half a dozen other French cities), organizes many sales each year in furniture, decorative arts, paintings and more, with some concentrating on objects of the twentieth century. I often discover desirable pieces by lesser-known French Art Deco and modernist designers here.

WRIGHT is a relatively new and newsy auction house in Chicago that specializes in twentieth-century design, art, and even residential architecture. They recently auctioned off a house by renowned architect Louis I. Kahn. Because Wright specializes in modern design, it often gets access to important furnishings through dealers that have not dealt with the older establishments.

ANTIQUE SHOWS

Going to a good antique show can be as informative as going to a museum with a decorative arts collection or attending an auction house seminar. Dealers are specialists and will be pleased by visitors' interest and happy to field questions about design, workmanship, and provenance. Experts from museums and auction houses are usually called upon to vet objects for the best shows, so authenticity is assured.

On the second day of a show, dealers will generally have more time to chat, once opening benefits are behind them and steady clients have had their go at the booths. Show catalogs can be used as future price guides for categories of furnishings that interest you. Leave business cards with dealers and ask to be put on mailing lists.

The **WINTER ANTIQUES SHOW** at Manhattan's Park Avenue Armory, going strong for more than fifty-five years, is the doyenne of fancy antique exhibits on the East Coast. There are seventy-five exhibitors, including specialists in American, European, Scandinavian, Russian, and Chinese wares.

The **AVENUE-WENDY SHOWS** are a series of family-managed, top-drawer antique exhibitions in New York, four at the Park Avenue Armory, and one in Morristown, New Jersey. They each feature over seventy dealers showing French, English, and Continental furniture from the seventeenth century through the Art Deco period. Eclectic displays overlap traditional antiques and contemporary art, and more conventional pieces rub up against the avant-garde.

The **STELLA SHOWS** are edgy and eclectic. The group sponsors an assortment of New York events; some are either strictly antiques or all-modern, and others merge antiques with outsider art and vintage clothing. They also organize a fair at Chicago's Botanic Garden that focuses on antique garden ornaments, tools, and accessories.

The **PALM BEACH WINTER ANTIQUES SHOW** features one of the most diverse groups of dealers and items of the highest quality. It's simply one of the best of its kind.

The **BIENNALE DE PARIS**, Paris's most prestigious antique show, hosts more than 100 dealers under the glass dome of the Grand Palais. All venerable French houses participate, among them **BERNARD STEINITZ**, known as the "Prince of Antiques," and **VALLOIS**, which specializes in Art Deco furnishings and modern and contemporary sculpture.

The **WINTER FINE ART & ANTIQUES FAIR** in London, known as the **OLYMPIA** show, is now in its sixteenth season. Dealers from around the world exhibit exceptional examples of furniture, glass, ceramics, textiles, and more.

ANTIQUE FAIRS, SWAP MEETS AND OPEN-AIR MARKETS

I often joke that the only difference between treasure and junk is where you bought it. Of course, that's stretching it, but for the interesting and offbeat to add texture to an interior, you can score great finds in a regional fair or flea market. At such events it's best to take a freewheeling approach. Allow yourself to go with an open mind. As to flea markets, people either love or hate them—they can be hot, scruffy, and overwhelming. The secret is to take it slow and focus on just a few categories or key vendors.

Popular events allow you to experience the flavor of a town or a culture, a sampling of its color and excitement. You will have better success at these happenings if you have done your homework by training your eye at museums, a few big antique shows, and auction previews. Although you are more likely to find a bargain at a swap meet or outdoor market, there is a trade-off: at high-end shows and shops, you pay for the editing ability, expertise, and contacts of trusted veterans.

The **BRIMFIELD ANTIQUES SHOW** began in the 1950s, and is one of the largest and best-known in the country. Held three times a year in a rural Massachusetts town in the Berkshires, the six-day fair draws 250,000 visitors and 5,000 dealers. Doing business here is strictly cash and carry; you must cart away your purchases yourself. There's a convivial, carnival-like atmosphere, but serious dealers from up and down the East Coast come here to buy.

Sifting through the stalls at the **SAN FERNANDO SWAP MEET** is an enjoyable antidote to combing the tony design shops of Los Angeles. Go to this sprawling outdoor fair with no expectations, come home with a Murano glass chandelier.

In Manhattan, the famous Twenty-sixth Street flea market has sadly closed down. But treasures can still be found on weekends at the **HELL'S KITCHEN FLEA MARKET** on far west Thirty-ninth Street and at the **ANTIQUES GARAGE**, whose 100 dealers have also relocated to that area.

As I travel, I keep my eye open for regional antique shows and fairs in resort and vacation-home areas such as the Hamptons, the Berkshires, and Palm Beach. Local newspapers, posters, and word of mouth are good sources of information on these happenings.

International open-air markets offer goods you just will not find elsewhere. Here are a few of my favorites: **BEIJING'S PANJIAYUAN WEEKEND MARKET** is organized by trade and provenance, so silversmiths, for instance, are grouped together, as are the crafts of Northern tribesmen, those from Tibet, and so on. I have found esoteric ceramic Buddhas and stunning Mongolian opera coats, highly embroidered and trimmed in fur, which I've cut and pieced for pillows. In Cairo's **KHAN ALI-KALILI** open-air market, virtually unchanged since the fourteenth century, I've had great luck with embroidered goods and small inlaid tables. Istanbul's **GRAND BAZAAR**, or **KAPALI CARSI**, offers textiles, glass, metalwork and pure floral extracts. I like Thailand's **PHUKET JATUJAK FLEA MARKET** for carved and hand-painted objects and for silver. The **DJEMAA EL FNA** in Marrakesh, Morocco, is a spectacular open-air, daily market that offers entertainment (acrobats, snake charmers, and drummers) as well as esoterica like embroidered leather goods. At the **STREET MARKETS IN TANZANIA** I have found beautiful wooden objects like headrests, carved figures, and masks, which bring to mind the African influence on artists like Brancusi and Picasso.

SHOPS

What makes a good shopping sleuth is the ability to recognize prizes when you come across them. Your mind is like a database, and all that you have seen or that has touched you in some meaningful way is stored there. Repetition reinforces the identification process. It becomes easier with practice to pick out what is aesthetically pleasing, what is of value, and what might be worth owning because it speaks to you in a special way.

I have channeled my love of shopping into a career! My closets are bursting. Of course, I have the advantage of buying not just for myself, but for ongoing decorating projects. In your final analysis of whether to purchase an item, however, it's important to remember to be particular because the goal is to build a meaningful collection. It's not about accumulating goods per se. It's about acquiring knowledge and appreciation, and learning to express oneself by building a decor with things that hold personal significance. Below, I share a few of the lesser-known names from my Little Black Book.

ANTIQUE AND VINTAGE SHOPS– In Manhattan, a couple of my favorite downtown antique shops are **MAISON GERARD**

for French and American Art Deco furniture, lighting, and *objets*; and **KARL KEMP** for nineteenth-century neoclassical styles and Biedermeier furniture. In the Hamptons, my choice is **YOUNGBLOOD** in Sag Harbor for owner Susan Yungbluth's personal taste in antiques, art and lighting. In Los Angeles, at **DRAGONETTE**, where the specialty is twentieth-century objects, I have gotten great buys on works by individual designers, like Tommi Parzinger silver coffee services. In Palm Beach, I like to prowl along the **DIXIE HIGHWAY**, known as Antiques Row, which packs about thirty-five shops, two restaurants, and a tearoom into a mile-long stretch.

I am attached to a couple of Copenhagen's streets, **BREDGADE AND RAVNSBORGGADE**, for vintage Scandinavian wares, and I've built relationships there with sources for pieces I've seen at important antique shows elsewhere.

In London, **PIMLICO ROAD** is where I go to get a look at as many antique shops as possible in a short span of time.

In Paris, I adore walking along **RUE DE L'UNIVERSITÉ AND RUE DE LILLE**, browsing at antique stores and other small home stores where proprietors with refined taste have made no-fail selections, often artfully integrating the old and the new. There is also the **LOUVRE DES ANTIQUAIRES**, a mall of about fifty fine antique stores just to the north of the Louvre Museum.

DESIGN STORES – In New York, one of my favorites is the seventh floor of **BERGDORF GOODMAN**, with its finger-on-the-pulse offerings. Grouped into areas by designer or style, the wares can encompass old hotel silver, items from a tasty estate sale, or a line of great new ceramics. A West Village shop where the proprietors also have an infallible sense of style is (the unpronounceable) **MXYPLYZYK**, with its good-value roundup of small contemporary furnishings (scaled to the limited square footage of the place) that run the gamut from toothbrush holders to ottomans and area rugs. An easily overlooked source for the occasional accessory with good bones and historical resonance is the **METROPOLITAN MUSEUM GIFT SHOP**. Don't miss the invaluable prints on the shop's second floor—framed and unframed reproductions of works by all the masters are for sale.

In Los Angeles, I always take a pass along La Cienega, popping in at **DOWNTOWN** for mid-century modern articles, fireplace accessories, and Venetian glass and **ROBERT KUO** for his original decorative objects with organic roots and an Asian sensibility.

I never stop in Paris without checking out a couple of Left Bank haunts: **AGNÈS COMAR** for her beautiful textiles, accessories and pillows; **GALERIE GLADYS MOUGIN** for contemporary furniture in steel, copper and bronze. In Venice, **TESSITURA LUIGI BEVILACQUA** is a magnet for me, a 300-year-old, family-run, specialty textile manufacturer for their superb damasks, brocades, and animal-print silk velvets. In Copenhagen, I keep current on modern classics at **ILLUMS BOLIGHUS**, the central, all-inclusive design shop, and can't resist stopping at **ROYAL COPENHAGEN** for classic and contemporary porcelain figurines and tableware.

ACKNOWLEDGMENTS

There are a number of people I would like to remember for helping me make this book a reality. All have contributed to this project as well as to my experience as a designer.

Pamela Fiori is not only a friend, she is a great mentor. I count myself both privileged and lucky to have her in my life. Pamela has inspired and guided me in organizing events that were among the most memorable to me, both professionally and socially.

Andrea Monfried, for celebrating my vision and signing me on to Monacelli's stable of talent. Jill Cohen, who was the first person to be shown the concept for the book and who made the proposal tangible and doable. Doug Turshen, for whom I have such respect as an artist and who makes something beautiful even better. Liz Gaynor, who paints with words as others do with watercolors. Everything becomes vibrant and clear.

George Ross, for being so clearly in tune with my vision. Our points of view are so perfectly aligned. I love the way you see everything as a tableau. Lilian Mishaan and Mathilde de Gutt, for the lessons on style and for committing to the vision.

Special thanks as well to: Seth and Jennifer Miller, Matt and Julie Anne Edmonds, Billie and Debbie Bancroft, Steven Tanger, Douglas Hannant, Frederick Anderson, Hutton Wilkinson, Beth de Woody, Margaret Russell, Anita Sarsidi, Candice Sutnick, Antonia Trimarchi, Gale Abrams, Amy Berman, Christine Belich, Fernando Bengoechea, D. D. Ryan, Sarah Medford, Dara Caponigro, Linda O'Keeffe, Patrick McMullan, Harry Maurer, Marjorie Miller, Meyer Russ from House & Garden, The Trump Organization, Sony International, and the Kips Bay Boys & Girls Club Decorator Show House.